Of the Map
That Changes

Of the Map That Changes

William Hunt

THE **SWALLOW PRESS** INC.

CHICAGO

Published by
The Swallow Press Incorporated
1139 South Wabash Avenue
Chicago, Illinois 60605

This book is printed on 100% recycled paper

ISBN (CLOTHBOUND) 0-8040-0623-7
ISBN (PAPERBOUND) 0-8040-0624-5
LIBRARY OF CONGRESS CATALOG CARD NUMBER 73-1503

New Poetry Series No. 46

Grateful acknowledgement is made to the following
publications in which many of these poems first
appeared:

*The American Scholar, Big Table, Chicago
Review, Choice, Epoch, Kayak, Michigan
Quarterly Review, The Nation, New, The
New Yorker, North American Review,
Perspective, Poetry, Poetry Northwest,
Quixote, and The Young American Poets.*

"This is a way," "The ladder you offer," "After a
fine day we found this," "Through the trees," "Two
days," "An exclusion of the stars," "Winter indoors,"
"Of the map that changes" first appeared in *Poetry.*
"How it might be" first appeared in *The New Yorker.*

For Marjorie

CONTENTS

I

II

III

IV

I

TWO DAYS

Across earth shadow moves like ants:
The clouds are being drawn
and drained away by the mountain.

Earlier when I watched through the smoke
of leaves on fire—smoke
with the glass breath of insect wings—
I was not watching, but bending down
to be bent.

At night there is a bird voice
that pulsates like a slowed heartbeat.
I wasn't listening near the end.
The red section of light at the backdoor
made me want to tell an old, old story:

That door would lead into a temple
crowded in its furthest room.
But I was cold because I waited
and in that inner room faces waited.
I cannot have them speak now.

Wind on the wild wheat like steam
in the morning below us. Then at four
there was thin rain and the third rainbow
of the week. It faded in the north
above the pines and Montefellonico
I felt something stooped
with dumbness as I threw out the trash.
Rainbows fade so
that you are not sure when they go.
You can blink and cause their return
for a while. Or bend your head.
At midnight I go out again.
Fog rises so that the moon's fall appears
to the east. The clothes I might wash
cannot be set out to dry.

AFTER A FINE DAY WE FOUND THIS

On a fine day . . . almost any
sort of song makes itself heard
Hölderlin

Whether we looked or not, with a glance
we knew of this again.
With eyes dim in the dusk, we could smile,
the day done away with. How far we came
and our host stood at the window
as if in the moon.

We did not hear a word spoken.
But later we talked of roads and buildings
and no one believed what was heard.

Poppies glowed within the field of wheat.
The town was not far from the garden.
We were watching our shadows,
on the yellow ground, they would not move
and so we turned and it was nightfall.
The worst began to happen. We watched
as the candle burned when handed to us,
and the glass overturned. We were in

the darkness and the other guests appeared
more alive than ever we had known them.

It is our life to know the lives of others,
to know even our life as another's and answer
when called. We have been a conversation,
but soon we shall be song. Then fireflies
came where there had been poppies.
Theirs was an absence of darkness
that left a popping, which (when blue)
is silent. Then a toast was given
to America. Striped field, stars loosened.

At the gate, while leaving, we looked for a child
and his mother that another guest also searched for.
"Everything takes place backwards here," he said.
We were also puzzled, unable to remember
(the moon set almost as soon as we arrived)
and so we spoke of death as an exhaustion of speech.

HOW IT MIGHT BE

How it might be to another: there is
your life I might know, but only when completed
(as a young girl you awoke with hollowed bones,
your hair chained to a rainstorm, while I bent
upon the damp wall outside your castle prison.)

This night is damp, only two thin lights show
from Montefellonico and the rain is pin-like
and now turns to snow. A blue flake flicks
from the light switch as I start up to bed.

A series of scenes exists where a saint walks up
and drifts down a mountain. Two villages are
set up like fans. Up close their walls are hollow.
"Watch out for mice," you said on the battlements
of Castiglione del Lago. The lake was a flat sky.
The farm's groves passed through the walls.

At our home mice are at home in our stove.
It is spring since we grew sick in Rome.
When I torture dreams the mice bathe in warm milk.
"When he turns pale I will resemble
a veterinarian," I said in my sleep.
The saint's jog is pictured in the electric flicker
of day-in, day-out. I wanted to lie in the peaceful storm
that would be you as a child, but I grew pale
as the current leapt from the stone wall of clouds.

Even if we are one, or two, interchanged,
or the same, with a signal of breath to recognize
the other after life, or after this series of lives
in a drift (which you will get) of stars, tonight
there are no stars. But there are those lights
that cross the veils of rain or snowfall, fan-like
with the trouble of dreams. We try to escape to each
other and are not ourselves. Before turning off the light
I lifted the stove's lid and saw the red eyes
of the mouse. He crouched full of another life.

THE WHEEL SEEN AT THE EDGES

Above all, those who did not, could not believe, return
and are friends. Their lives change beneath these waters.
As we planned to leave, the car I knew would be buried in sand.
Three suicides almost returned like shore waters under light:
Friends that are a black door we open and turn away from.
Like those steps we slip down in dream in order to waken
and I thought aloud: I want only to sleep and it all die:
water, colors of water, friends who are light, beliefs
that were forms of doubt with feet and arms. In sand
the wheels turned to no purpose. Shore waters
returned shed of purpose, faces return beneath backwash.

These are my arms, my feet, also my voice.
How many flowers in the foam, how many petals
in the spray of sand as the car wheel turns?
The wide beach of bathers shudders with that song.
How old bathers grow in the sunlight and the wind
under the trees is as under a god's stiffened arm.

I hardly knew. These spaces are known aloud!
The dead speak of them: *We made mountains for you
to stumble.* But deep down where there is no day
they stumble also, answering by the sound of their feet.
That sound is their name.
It is not the dead that come back; we return.
Moving between mountains I see them. I saw them
and do not believe that they were more than water.
A broken mirror of light coming back,
they took shape. They stumbled in the hall.
After I opened the door and turned away,
I was the one who fell, but like an old man
whose beliefs were his own jokes about mountains.

9

The bathers surrounded the stalled car. The song rose
and the bathers brought wood. Mountains rose.

I can escape your disbelief, your half life of light
that speeds across water and yet is broken.
If I knew more the sands would be a quiet flame.

For the bathers our leaving became an abrupt game;
the mountains were small and the waves tired.
The waves removed themselves at intervals and since then
we have all gone away, but the door was left open
and our dead friends stumble at the edges of things.

OUT OF TOUCH

When it rains here the toads
come out on the roads,
and they do not avoid
what hurtles toward
them, what cannot move aside
in the fog, the headlights a white
bath. While the toad looks up
his back's curve is that of a man's
(while he does push-ups),
but his hands are more deliberate.

And after midnight, blue snails
fall from the backdoor with
the sound of stones hollowed out.
The moon presses into clouds
so that a form of rainbow surrounds
it. I step outdoors and am
placed in these distant wounds.

The animals near to us here
are heedless. Weather-
stripping a door my scissors awoke
two scorpions who would not touch.
They would be men if mushrooms
were trees. The cold moves the cold-
blooded like bits of dust that
cling to a finger. This poem
has no ending. It is not smart
enough to cross roads.
It would climb up closed doors.
It is drawn out of hiding
by the rain in me. It stares
at the road and keeps its place.

11

WE BEND

We bend in the first rains that we know.
Our feet hurry at nightfall as if to school.
We were talking about your name. Why
did you answer? The train is beneath the hill.
It's the one we would have taken before.
Now we are up to our knees from a distance.
Someone counts flowers, but not us.
That was never us. Who should tell the rest?
It is not good to be so long ago. Looking down
you'll know that and wave from a moving window.

THE LADDER YOU OFFER

And some too have been saved
as though on lovely islands.
                    Hölderlin

When we are this close to the waves
they are a prison which moves—
the small stones run out with the tide.

On my knees
I wanted to correct how the air flames
in the green hollow of the stone
which is water
for a moment. We have been elsewhere
and space is also much like being young:
the stars waver on each veil,
the curtains that we see through,
and it being still hidden.
We called.

This is not home. By the waters,
black sand, our auto facing outward,
pastel office buildings, too late
now for a sunset.
How easily the voice hardens to describe.
Black sand: a shoe box fills with you to drown.
Sunset: a hand fills with you to bathe.
There are no further stories of the dead.

Other than these:
There was talk of fate: a drum beat.
But we argued that night about whistles.
Laughter over voices becoming those of birds.
A presence separating the limbs of the poplar,
and at dawn another grasping of wheels
over gravel, by the shoreline, bells.
We had stopped talking, to make it safe.

It must keep on, you know,
like the ladder you pointed out in the sky.
What made you think of that?
Parts of my body do not like me.
My knees think that they are a face,
my eyes move your arms toward mine.

At least the sun won't rise again,
that is the last word in all catalogues.
Many others have watched this
and had the sense to keep silence.
So close to the water, thinking of prison,
the ladder you offer, the stars also.

SO THAT WOMEN WILL TALK TO TREES

So that women will talk to trees often at midnight,
the cat rubbing their white-gowned and chilled legs,
so that this will occur when I am dead,
I talk to trees now. They say,
> Our roots are not arms,
> our limbs are fastened on,
> but caught up in
> violence with the wind.

There is no discussion when air fills with seeds:
> It is our bridal day and wedding night
> shared throughout the world. Wind and rain
> are an aid. I asked of the insects.

The trees in that autumn would only recall birds
and compared their grace to their own wind-blown seed.
Like a lonely wife, its dream returned to its yearly youth,
the messages of wildly driven sex,
reminiscent also of the tidal motionings of the sun.
The door opens. The cat precedes the woman
to the tree. Where am I?
The door into the tree opened long ago,
all that has been said by the tree I said and say again
to the woman who sits in the white gown of the moonlight.

WE RAN

We ran on a dark path beside the lake.
We could hear the oars of boats
and laughter. We wanted to be lost.
I recall that you were undressed.
Then I was stopped by the moon.
We were buried in the light of ghosts.
So many years have passed,
hospitals and loneliness for you.
Seated that night, our legs crossed.
How will it happen, that moon's setting?

AND NOW WE HAVE LEARNED

And now we have learned these songs
have no end, have no voice, have no
no. In them the street is lit but silent;
there is the chimney's breath, the movement
of dry goods on a counter, and the flaring
of nerves toward the barriers of light.
By the stone bench I recall what I missed:
the child following the child following . . .
the next step should involve the moon
and all the sleep we neglected.
But when shall we remember this lamplight,
the sweetness of wet leaves,
and the children damp in their voices?
A child holds up a hand and cries
to us. I have hidden from the moon to learn
crawling. It is not the full moon that hurts;
it is the fullness of its tired night.

WE ARE THE BODY OF SONG

I. *Living in Space*

As we tilt the sunlight separates into diamonds,
cold oil elevates a surface of crystals. Space
cries: a surface of crystals slides in liquids.
In refraction the houses of night once lost
are found. Each of our thoughts repeats
how the horizon repeats its white band of cloud.
As we tilt lakes glisten like rain in fire.
This distance is a stomach of fullness. Space
is that part of my chest. The earth becomes
my broken hand, without pulse, seen close
you see only shadow and light of blood
as we tilt.
                    It could not be this cold
and yet when Asia's lake fires thin beams
they are warm as souls, voices, a possible blue.
My flesh is that of yours, its hills and the sun
set everywhere as I tilt beneath the black table.
Sun burial on the Pacific link. Soiled drift
locked in by the pressures of my head: slides
leg us as we repeat.

How many windows, layers of snowed light
before space grows too large? I count
as we tilt. Sunlight, coiled in a stomach's
serpent. Sunlight, cold oil in crystals
slides in the chutes of the snowflake. Space,
the night fills with the sad fronds of our wings.
Our shoulder blades cut into love and birth fireworks.
The stomach when it is clouds, when it is
at the edge of conception, when dust blown

on the walls circles inward to the wheel
as we may fall. The pathway, the repetition
of cloud we imagined three days ago
within this house of night and find the labyrinth
of the bed tighten as a limp-flowered wing
of Asia, the broken glass
holding flame. It is the cold of the skeleton
that turns a possible blue and edges to the
black table. Space, may it grow large or small,
marred, or a woman's hair in fountains on
my flash of love, seen in the light of blood,
there is no thought you need. Hum of
warmed steel, needles of the atom, cold
skeletons of the sun, many stars
repeated in the bowl. We run the black table.
As we tilt, in the cold, we do not believe
and chastened by wings slow as a life lived
in bed when we once awake.

II. *Night Space*

Thin, we are a speck tracing the travelers,
arms outstretched, followed by fire's cloth,
Phaeton by Cetus from Orion and the knife.
The gods cannot see. We emend their map
and the wind does not change. Our path
the click of light clocks.

On another day:
a man bears water (Phaeton reaches), the fish
pressed gives water (the man turned away).
He rides on the black and crowded sea.
Here is the secret hunt. The spilled fireplace,
Scorpio rising, the wolf impaled and silence.
We enter on the broken path, at times.
Our eyes shut tight, we want the scales,
the crown to dangle. The wind does not grow.
Only silence of the nerve's tree and bloom.
We're caught and over the wheel what resembles
a pool of cloud. Spokes, needles guide us
through the centaur's shield and breast.

On time
the boat awaits us, above to the right
the Hydra's winged passenger. We move
through it, an electric palimpsest, the great
yellowing dog, an ocean liner without oars, sails,
or propeller, going toward the green hare,
who rests beside Orion and the clothed fire.
25° and we began to fall, under the fish, beneath
fire, hooves, the broken wake through the blue
cloud that we imagined three days before. Now
gathering arms close in our path to the center,
like a glove turned inside out. We are shook free
like a hand out of foliage when clocks are life itself.

THE OWL HAND

> *A child who with its eyes bandaged had*
> *lost several of its fingers by amputation,*
> *continued to complain for many days successively*
> *of pains, now in this joint and now in that,*
> *of the very fingers which had been cut off.*
> Biographia Literaria

And when he slept this child's hand grew,
each finger stalk-like, tipped
with a dark nail whose curve resembled
that of the degenerate Khans. He gripped
the sides of his body, his thighs shuddered
like a bird caught in a change of wind:
The soft bones were not there. Then
the bird that grew at the edge of his finger tips
began to talk. "You," he said and disappeared.
There was an itch in the replica of the *mons veneris*
that he recognized lay in his middle finger.
For him the Mount of Venus was a death trap
complete with ax and the curse of the Pilgrims,
progress. As he slept his fingers wove the delicate
wing jointures of the bird one by one
and his mouth was a cone of heavy bone,
and his voice once shrill was deep
as it whispered, "You," and struggled to escape.

MY CHILD DREAMS

My child dreams of the birth of snow
and this is the earth where snowflakes gather.
At night all the doors to my house open.
Sea, hill and wood, the town fills with people!
and the dead pause to hear their hearts beat.
Earlier I thought the snowfall careless of love—
they are travelers who know only the wind.
For a long while they do not fall. The stranger,
the child, enters us through doors of snow and fire,
the rose of ice, the hollow wound and the opened sea.

II

AUTUMN IN THE PLAINS

Lying on your back in the chill of November
the map of the sky seems incomplete.
Through the trees there are only the stars.
In the well you would see them again.
In the blue house, that the moon surrounds,
the porchlight is like a bending head.
My wife is indoors singing to the cats.
Above the house the stars throb
as if I only partially watched them.
The cold ground makes me forget my bones.
On the trees what leaves are left
threaten to tear away suddenly.

WHAT YOU CAN GET FROM THE BODY

You can get all of the soul out of the body.
It rises like a corpse would from a lake's bottom,
slowly but obedient to natural law.
It is in a purple or possibly a blue
elevator shaft. Through the dense roar
of the water it calls your floor.

Except for the feet which will rest
in the eye sockets, as in stirrups,
while you want the soul to escape entirely,
it will only bend over forward,
precariously perched under your eyelids
facing a torrential rain. The soul wears a hat
and guards its face from the wet.
When you are blind it is free to remove its shoes
and run away over and over again.

THIS IS A WAY

This is a way to be alone, I thought,
but I did not love it.
Somewhere beneath the grey branches
there was a stream.
But the branches hid it like a net.
I preferred the young poplars nearby.
If I had laid down in ivy
(I must have once)
then at that moment I would have gone.
I stayed to watch.
I smelled the water.
We are supposed to know where we live.
But we always look around.
Now, I'm looking down in these branches,
imagining insects, mostly beetles
that are red and phosphorescently green,
and that the frogs are sleeping.
A god must have led me here bit by bit.
I can still hear my feet arriving.
They drag in the mud beside the poplars.
A whole group of us meet.
We lean watching the confusion
of branches that hide this stream.
A god would spare us this leaving
but there is corruption
and the next step should be a sleep.
I could do that, if I was truly alone,
and when I awoke I would look up
through the poplars,
my thoughts fresh as on a marriage day.
I'd be a cold cup of water
clear enough for you to see yourself in.

AN ENTRANCE INTO THE WATER

The meadow and the moon:
my silence and your entrance

into the waters of light,
or so I think of your arms
and hear a voice that says,
"More and more darkness
is where she hides
behind the stalks of grass."
How could you hide
and I hold you also?
Tonight again I am
prepared to die—
clumsy as a young girl,

you swim beyond the dockside,
but all memories prepare us
for death as a woman dressed
in black and with fins.

The flattened leaves of the lake's
surface shift and somewhere below
is your swim-suited flesh, chilled

and I miss making you more warm
than you have ever been.
It is like the weight
of a drowned body, loving
this way, that we carry
wearily onto the shore and also
there is the meadow and the moon.

BEHIND THE HOUSE, BETWEEN THE NIGHT WIND

The thin reds of the lawn
drain and the man sits in his blackened shoes
and in the flat sheets of the wind.
The night fits into a closet.

The backdrop of black pines
locks in place with the sky.
The woman leans on the house,
her arms crossed, in a white and gray house dress
She waits for something to rebel.

The man holds onto a stone
with the violet pockmarks of old bone.

The dog listens to the growths
between the sections of the wind.
His head nods up and down.
Once, long ago the man wanted to throw
the stone. The grass leans completely
across the field. It slices the shadows.
In his wrist the stone is a delicacy of weight.
The world is being divided
and handed out to the living.
But in the stone a man whispers to the dog.

OF WHAT IS TO COME

We are still walking across the lawn.
"How sad you are, when you should be,"
she said. We watch the whitened house,
the door suggests details neglected in dreams
and there is a window which is dark.

We appear to be walking across the lawn.
Trees await us like an ornate picture frame.
"Atlantis will levitate to sea level by 1998."
She spoke with her face broken by the shade.
That is how a woman sometimes enters a forest.

We are still as is a lawn before its house.
The woman pulsates captured by thin tree limbs:
this is the way the stars breathe in and out.
It is like daydreaming without a dream.
Here is the window and there was the lawn.

THE MESSAGE

A moth's brown wings open on the ceiling.

There is another half to my life. It is
webbed with the rain's weight in the trees.
A man watches this darkened window and leaves.
He picks white flowers in the white rain light.

My wife sleeps folded in the way of the fallen.
Her slender legs glow against her breathing.
Outside someone is calling someone indoors.
I enter the world through the blonde bodies
of women undressing. The motioning of trees
suggests such a woman's gestures. Night time.

I search the window before I leave. Something
like a mirror breaks. Now there is the dense
warmth of shame and of the intimate.
The moth's body of dust thickens the shadows.
How long have I been outdoors calling this way?

THE TREES BEFORE NIGHTFALL

Next week there would be your voice
past the window and the line of trees
where you hid. The warmth searches me.
You are dead to this world. All those towers,
those trees belong to wings that shredded
to dust-green gowns. Once the feathers
clutched each other. Now the dust rises.
This is the beginning of the darkness:
the leaves gathering in and silence
force us to our feet beneath the moon.
Afterwards we speak of circles, walks,
your eyelids bruised from unbroken windows.

AN EXCLUSION OF THE STARS

With the sound I no longer know now behind me,
it should have been
wind scrambling through oak trees when I was five,
or you, my new wife, singing with your arms
unsheathed from the shoulders of a white dress.

Your thin body's pallor:
the cloud-lit sky that precedes rainstorms. At midnight
that sound was neither music nor death.
The foliage was part of the tearing and weaving
of the child. He clambers through the green trees
swimming to the blackened roof of the forest.

Once the trees were quiet,
but the boy rises through the clatter of breaking branches,
and the trickle of moonlight becomes rain falling.
You, my wife, are part of the rainstorm
once further away than the moon.

These words separate us into sound;
the panels of light on your arms, and your arms also,
hold us together:
these systems, these choices:
the child, the woods (the wife, the storm)
exclude what I would have said otherwise of the stars.

A GROUPING OF DARK ROOMS

I

I wrote you a letter once before it rained.
The fog horn imitates grey flowers wrung dry,
goodnight. The insomniac learns
that his head is the moon. He is upset
in his rooms, occupied
with the burial of knees and of toes.

II

Poems are about the mapping of rain:
at each moment we have the complete record.
The garden of the old maid laps our walk.
The tulips died overnight, or were never there.
At dinner time her mother stood there in the fog.
Go home, I prayed, as I drove home.
Her daughter ran from a grouping of dark rooms
to her mother tilted against the rain.
Our map ends at this point twice.

III

It rains tonight and once all week.
It does what?
Her mother tosses aside the foliage of torn maps.

IV

Three maps show tree-green rain patterns.
The other is of the night. I am satisfied.
Meanwhile, our house lights, our door locks.

The caption for the moon remains incomplete,
It's a threat: Next time walk in your sleep.
So I did. It is no better than the life of tulips.

V

What's better than fog? There has to be,
but what about driving home too fast?
I wrote you to send you this map, now it rains.
The tulips were brought in to dry. It rains
now even more so while you are safe asleep.
By the way, the lost part of the map reads:
As the moon is alone now, so were we all once.

CLARK STREET

Upstairs a Puerto Rican took his life
today at half-past noon. Five cops led his wife
away in a beige car. Her lament was more foreign
than we could feel and was there blood on her hand,
the way she held it to her stark red hair?
It was as if something wrong was not there.
The fire escapes tremble delicately, stiffly sunlit.
The red hair of the wife submerged in the dark traffic.

THE UNEASY FOLIAGE

The uneasy foliage of the trees
hides a gesture which cannot awake.
This is of our confusion about wives
while our children play beneath statues.
The children are armed with their laughter.
Watching, we live the lives a statue imagines.
A wife speaks of passages and doorways.
The children scatter and dare us to describe
mystery. Talk to them in their sleep.
They are fixed in position like the leaves.
My wife raises my shoes and they are filled
with white stones. Only the statue is awake.

THE ASTRONAUTS ENTER CHICAGO
ARM IN ARM WITH THE VICE-PRESIDENT
OF THE U.S.A. ON FLAG DAY, 1965

Half asleep petals of the storm rub together,
green and white calyx of leaf lightning, blue and white
breasts evaporating. Darkening on all fours
the black cars, teaching our morals a dance:
the drum majorettes. Fathers in the shade,
sunlight on their wives, on the slender boys,
white knees and lips of the daughters,
listening to recorded music.
Lean families against the sun.

The batons rise into the storm.
The close-shaven heads of the heroes
bend to the right and to the left like new wheat.
They have the smile of those who have never lost.
The storm oppresses the insects,
drugged with the cold they crawl in air-conditioned offices,
grasshoppers blow over the green oil-slicks of Calumet Harbor.
Tears rise in the eyes of young women
as the vice-president's arms rise against the sky.

MUSIC IN MICHIGAN

The blind vets hear music from the darkened lakeside,
voices from autos, and they visualize the thin
limbs of the water and of the swim suits.
In Vietnam her left arm burst from the shoulder,
dark as burnt candlewick, it moved on the ground.
"I am too old now to understand why this occurred,"
she said. Too late, the moon drawn upon a string
sets. Too late to see the young dance in Michigan.
The blind men rock in time to the shore waters.
Their fingertips grow out toward the water.
An animal's breath passes within their reach.
The moon was the memory of windows
to which the children of the poor say prayers.
Whispering into its wings the owl simplifies
the search for the lost arms of the living.

DEAD END ROADS

I

Crickets clung to the stone wall indoors
and to save their lives I broke their legs.

II

He rose like a pillow into my headlights.
And as I braked he passed under the right
fender. As in a repeated dream I backed
up and drove over the tracks of the possum.
On my hands and knees I searched for his blood.
Watch how his ghost waddles on the light's edge.

III

The sun on the bed held birds beneath clouds.
But the long hallways were grey with feathers,
lighter than dust to a broom, and the cats slept.

IV

The rain shredded the surrounding lamplight.
We were like maniacs at the flashing windows
as a dead tree fell and filled with mushrooms.

V

In November I made plans to sleep outdoors.
The animals sleepwalk to their unknowable sacrifice.
At the screen the racoons hovered with rubbery paws.
The length of the night grew and I assumed this voice.
It is a kindness to our lives to wait and fall asleep.
This is how I have learned that our ghosts require blood.
The animals help us. Hunched, they wait for a silence
sudden as a hand shook free from the foliage.

CALENDAR

I
Above the violet pond the crow calls
to the deeps in us, but with the wrong voice.
Two Fords parked by the front door.

II
She plays solitaire, plays with her child's
stare, plans her past, her stars and complains.

III
I lost something and came to look again.
In the garden was a handful of pills
and in the trees the violence of birds.

IV
Her head was averted in the silence
that the snow brings. The blue house stood.

V
The house accumulates weighthlessness the way
a man blacks out. At sundown it flies off.

VI
She turns to us the last card. A leaf flickers,
a Lincoln-green moth rises, the underside
of its wings white as the first snowfall.

NEW DEATH: INCEST

The moon holds a father with two legs
by the iron of jaws on the blued sand
and by the arms holds child songs:
the child in his arms is his own.
Aged three, aged ten, aged thirteen.
In her throat he turns over,
a slow motioning somersault.
As he dives through her fountain hair,
he breaks her arms, her voices
of women on the peonie horizon.
He falls further, past her hand-sized heart,
windows filled with dry goods, dust-
green shirts, and the beach-drying light
of the moon god, a dense red.

THERE IS THE ROAD

There is the road I have not filled,
although each day I speak of it.
On it each day I must drive slower.

On the high ground past the laurel
a child is herding swine.
She folds her arms and smiles.

The dirt road needs to be filled.
Each day the car lurches in it deeper.

To admit these things
is to speak of indifference.
How should the road stay in place?

The young girl leans back
as if she might spend
her entire life in the field.

I have seen her close.
Her eyes are spaced so widely
to remind me of the stars at night.

She leans back as does the grass,
but each time that I hear the wind
it is more quiet near where she stands.

Newton told of how the stars
press together, but do not touch.
All wetness suggests the carnal,
the rain and the fall of stars.

The sows cross the broken road.
The folds beneath their tails
close off a door onto this world.

The child looks down from a wheel.

GOING UPHILL

Now comes the time when I can find no excuse,
yet I get drunk nightly. Up the hill I would
enter the storm. The rain is an endless gown
that sweeps through the distant porchlights.
It's spring and I have fallen among mushrooms.
My body is like an empty glass as it spins to us.
The clouds slip apart and move the purple grass:
smoke and fire. I enter where fever fills
the eyelids and I spiral in the violet's birth.

SONG FROM THE END OF THE EARTH

Deny and what will be given you?
Sunlight on the rose bush, a breeze
on the green bronze gong of the pond,
a breeze sifting the thorns,
with invisible birds on white wings.
Deny the sun and you are fed to dreams,
a procession of beasts:
the blood-filled eye.
Deny the moon and you are given cathedrals,
spires, skeletons, death on wings;
the amputated arms of Hermes,
his marble stare, green tundra.
Deny the wind and you become deaf;
the wings twist within cloud;
the door is shut, the clock is stopped:
these windows give out onto death.
Deny water and sun sets.
Deny fire and the breath becomes landscape,
hollyhocks tacked on the closed door:
the lion shall be small on this design.
Deny and you will be given children, a son.
Deny and you will grow large in more than shadow.
Deny and the wings will not be consumed in fire.

III

WINTER INDOORS

A friend comes from afar
and walks with me almost.

At noon the wheels disappear
over the top of the hill
with the sound of applause.
Who is this friend?

This world is cold as glass.
Ghosts return at times,
but even then stay in the past.

My awakenings are like rain
that beats on a dark window.

In the empty yard the blown rain
is almost a ghost or a man.
His face is turned away.
Across his back like whip marks
are the shadows of winter trees.

THE CUT-OFF

The knife on the table is a thought.
But so is the cup.

No one will awaken to tell you
what to remember.
Like an automobile
my friends pull out on the driveway.

A man stands by the lake;
in itself that is an afternoon.

Nearby is a picnic of friends,
their voices, cups and knives.
At night we will shake hands, kiss
and head to the deserted house.

NOAH BELOW ZERO

This must be the wintry weariness of Noah
that drove him against his wife, Uxor.

With dazzled eyes, Blake's Tyger curled up on the couch:
Our old cat licks his dry, furred-over bones.

Drawn awake from a nap, I have missed the sunset.
Slowly I catalogue the hallways of my arms and head.

They are littered with thin snow drifts, foliage.
The dead bird I found today in the street will sing there.

The old cat watches the bird's wings in the heel of my hand.
I do not have to do what I do not want to do.

I call my wife and build my ark,
resolving to fill it only with birds.

MY WORK WITH SNOW

My work with snow is crucial,
while yours, beautiful woman, is with water.
The part of me that is the wind
scatters the snow over the moon-deepened pond,
where I attempt to clarify these snow prints
of your lips and of your breasts.
You are evasive as roads that constantly fork.
Your virtue is of gently rising hills,
and your name, which I know by heart,
I call out as easily as the wind speaks at night.

THE BODIES OF SNOW ARE SLEEPY

It snowed and we took off our clothes
again and in the streetlight the snow
held the slowed perfection of rain
that might fall, but slower than our clothes.
We trembled.
(Held the slowed perversion of rain
that we might fall, but slower in our lives.)
The fire of snow is sent in white boxes.
White fire to unwrap and to undress.
While a voice whispers, "Go to bed."

ASKING AFTER YOU

When it is this cold we see double,
do you remember?

Your arm reflected on the window
and the white trees underwater,
where they darkened and flashed
from the rain gathered together.

We spun through the wet leaves
as if brown birds could chase us
and downhill there was more water
in a lake
that we could not look at.
I can now.
But why can't you?
Just because you left for good.
That is the reason.
Goodbye, till we meet again
and again.

WINTERING IN THE HEARTLANDS

The heart longs for a pickax.

At once off the ice, as if crippled,
each skater walks with his own style.
The lake horizon slit distinctly—
the long line between bodies pressed together.

Inside my shoes
a man curls up to sleep.
Again and then again curling around the sun.
His eyelids dark as green beetles
and maternal oceans.
Their delicate folds burnt shut.

This is a sketch from a child's primer,
where a hint of wind is made by three lines.
A row boat beached far back on the sand,
its hull the breast bones of a crow.
We're near the edge where the fire beckons.

The ice goes on into a distance that is blue
with the weight of the snow.
There the thin sail of an ice boat thumps the air
and tilts like a knife in slow motion.

WHAT REMAINS

At dawn what remains of sleep is snow.
On the lawn the birds repeat
the stiffened footprints that a dream has traced.
It is an ocean of blue leaves for a boy
to break through. He is the wind that moves
on the growth of clouds. There birds are buoys.

A tree limb is caught like a bird's foot.
It struggles and buries itself, back and forth.
How strange the cold is to the bones each snowfall.
The boy runs away from home to the store.

I did that once. Snow hollows out that search,
which was for a certain syrup. Twig prints,
the trail of birds, lie on the blue lawn.
I cannot recall how I got home. A bird stops
in mid-air. Its wings separate, frozen in space.

Now we see how each flake falls in single file.
The bird tilts above the crumpled wind.
The child's day prepares for a snowman.
But the snowman's dream is for a summer
of absolute zero. There we are still his servants,
stiffened as the brittle twigs of spilled syrup.

The earth has ended to become the sky.
Now, the boy runs to where the snow begins.
A boy hurried by. At his return
he will wave his arms to show that they are cold
and how a great labor has been done.

THINGS ARE ALWAYS BETTER INDOORS

The snowfall crosses the mirror.
The trees pull themselves back.
They dream they will go in hiding.

Where are the vivid genitals of the flower
that were shaped like a crutch?
Do they only seem scattered?

We walked single file on the ice,
our voices were broken leaves.

A fox listens for the heartbeat of fish.
Beneath him thin moons speed by.
The eyes of the fox are shrunken.

Once indoors we walk further indoors.
The gestures of the trees are permanent.

HOW IT GOT TOO COLD

Now the cat hurries through the moon.
My hand frees the mouse in her mouth.
The animal circles his own labyrinth.
He tracks a pink noodle of flesh;
extruding, the intestines stick to concrete.
The moon dives through snow quilting.

Red mouse eyes repeat the huddled curve of fur.
In him heartbeat and breathing become one.
We lock the cats in with tired eyes.
The males urinate against the white walls.

The skeletons of the moon
shiver upon the platforms of leaves.
This song for the dead mouse, the labyrinth.
In our chairs we are the animal's tombstone.

Now the cat, Lulu, hurries to her station.
Now the mouse choirs her on in a circle.
Never to have been born was a dream.
And now it has gotten too cold.

THE CIRCUIT OF ORION: CHAPTER TITLES

There was the title of a chapter we forgot,
while we spoke of how close it had gotten to where
we had come (or gone), for that night in the thin mountains
we fell asleep, and the closed door was otherworldly,
a thing we saw light at the edge of, only light and not
each time we looked. Your note would say it takes place
in darkness, but I imagine your note and your hand is a flame.
How badly we have all felt as if we had died
and still remain as our own mourners. *It is not bad*
is what your note would add and the flame not burn.

"Today, I walked toward the oak trees swiftly
and all the time I remember it I try to turn
around. Don't you try to remember now. No
image is what it was. Sunlight's that way also."

The Name is going too far, after all. *After
All* is better. When we spoke we were almost,
almost—and the mountains were not thin, but the wind
was asleep (or gone) like a closed door of sunlight
that we are the edge of, and seen as, but not
when you think it is wrong to turn. You start back.
In something like clothes you might have died
and now you start back with something like a moan,
which is what you said, or I imagine these words flare
in my hand as you walk swiftly to the oak trees,
and the image, when is it not a thing? but this voice
that won't, or will almost, and then forgot.

THROUGH THE TREES

Through the ragged wall of trees the sails!
They held the sunlight.

My fingers leaned with the sudden pain
of forming tents on my brother's lap.
The road turned more to the right
and had the gentle curve of a woman
who reaches far inland for mountains.

Through the long silver night in bed
we laughed and wrestled until my brother cried.
Nothing was left. We look out that window.

Because you are there the night is there,
mother of clouds. In the sleep of trees
the child's shadow glows. At the end
of the meadow, his legs are a fountain
that wants tears.

As if breathing, the moon
Unfolds the clouds, death.
The moon and the child's eyes
move to the window.
He listens for the trees.

YOUR LIFE AFTER DEATH

(For Harlan E. Hunt)

I

In their pot of golden tin-foil
the green-onion stalks of the hyacinth bend
under the weight of a non-existent wind.

Within the winter's heat of this house
they turn brown and give off that same odor
that bred behind our nursery radiator.

Aged twenty-six, my brother
lays in a blood-soiled porcelain tray,
his eyes squeezed to black lumps in three days.

Three days he lay face down
and alone until his death led the neighbors by the nose
to his locked door. He had curled up without his clothes.

II

You were in my first dream,
aged two then. You slept curled behind bars in a bib
and slept on while the three Gold Dust twins tickled my ribs.

This sleep or fall that I must fear. . .
for within it I take on your attitude in death.
My limbs are strange to me, intent on your death.

I see children everywhere.
Whiskey is easy to approach. Sleep is a box
of wood. Your foot is a white shoe bronzed on a block.

Or your foot in its turning out
bursts the white bindings. And your poor hands
won't come to mind. In death at first we expand.

We want to see you again.
After three weeks the hyacinth developed a serious lean-
ing over, but the stalks stayed green. They stayed green.

OF THE MAP THAT CHANGES

The music, I imagine, is for Harlan
who recalls what is to follow
(as the wind recalls the path it has chosen
tracking its own distortion through
the trees), even now as his death ends.
And the music is also yours. Marjorie,
my wife: that distention of trees tends
to have the voices of the animals we
love together. They attempt your name to call
you home. But you will not leave till we are done:
you are the way wind catches its breath. It falls
to its knees, like our sleep, before moving on.

All your dead now live. Your parents
and your sister live again (like the voices
that live in trees and which we hear in currents
that embrace the leaves and multiply choices).

Harlan has been reborn. He is two years old
and dwells in new and dark robes with new parents,
alone as we, in the Chinas of this world.
Needless as they are our fears for the dead rend
us with glimpses of beauty: attached to trees,
fears are the mist-fleshed dreams we add one by one,
each autumn, to take the place of falling leaves.
Marjorie, look, our dead are returned, they run
back toward us in the window wake of the moon
we searched after through the emptied, gloomy room
of that suburb tonight. We should search for them,
the dead, not as we once did by playing dead.
We shall look for the dead like those men who spread
their vision to hold both mountain and ocean:
they search for nothing and they are the chosen.

In his cradle my younger brother is older
than I, because of his death and his new life.
His aged face says our loves are negligible,
but final, imperfect as that of a wife.

Your arms move up and down in the darkened room.
You are left alone, this is victory, you wish
it left you yourself, like the erased mist
beyond which is found the changes of the moon.

CONCEPT OF THE ELECTRICAL BODY

Lightning would be a gathering of souls
crashing back to earth (in a great
pile-up of whitening
light); they fell from clouds,
tore into the tree's armies.

The frizzled leaves bulking the street
are a child's hair; blond motionings
of dimmed breathing.

The tree limbs twisted by the ghost-
strengthened arms: workmen,
the torsos of washerwomen naked to the waist,
pillars. The soul longing for nerves,
the plasticity of the veins which it has lost,
as also finger tips, genitalia,
through the effect of lightning
leaves a tracing of the desired body
through the shape of mountains, valleys,
pale feminine lakes.

How all the world longs to be a man
and a woman in love, loving
with the sullen build-up of threatened storms!
The bodies of the lovers struggle
throughout the night's storm to make their body.

LIMB BREAKING

The branch breaks in the river's direction.
The mirrored branch breaks. Birds talk.
Leaves flutter onto the breaking mirror.
The wound on the tree is a mirror at last softened.
The tree climber is pieces of glass and water drops.
Like the moon we hang onto the mangled limb.
If I break, then behind me, my cradle will rock.
I learned only one song: remember me, remember ...
Endlessly rocked: branch, river and the breaking.

MOTHS AT THE WINDOW

Our aunt's teeth become a skeleton's.
Moths are at the window, jewels of horror
and memory. Furniture is falling.
My relatives argue above the death bed.
They are like a child with long hair,
who holds a candle and smiles.
Hidden behind dust-brown wings,
you read it in her weary eyes.
It is Aunt Mary they snuff out.
Her grin surfaces with the bone.

A SONG FOR GREGOR SAMSA

When young the child
closes its eyes, will not look at things;
it is a long time before it speaks.
The symbol of the search on both knees,
the memory it has when it cries
in the dark, we shouldn't forget,
nor remember too much the sunlight
on the swing, the green flowers on the wall,
bedtime at twilight, the music from down the hall,
nor the song which will make us a child,
the moment we wave our arms
haphazardly and close our eyes.

THIS IS THE DAWN, THIS IS THE STORM

My head leans further into the maple's foliage.

The tree's roots are the amputated arms of Hermes.
His hand curves to force me forth.

Oceans of grass fold back stealthily:
spirits with feet thin as whistles.

The storm passing with its gathering of the dead,
the trees, the grass and my breath bend over.

DOWNSTREAM WITH THE OTHERS

We love the other divers only
while they are in mid-air. The swim
and the rest we still share, it's
almost a voice that undresses us,
it calls with the snowflake's
stiffened grace and falling.

How warm the underwater becomes
as you rest entering the harbor.
The waves there are yellow,
breaking the windows along the shore.

Touching, there are only rivers:
it is the lesson of the bird
that passes over the river,
it is the lesson of the snowstorm
that passes invisibly into the river.

IV

VI

AN INVITATION

Similar to those exhausted dreams of lost gardens,
my thoughts are of you hand in hand with children,
and of voices that I did not know I owned
(they approach us like a dark band of horses at dawn)
tentative with sorrow and the moon-distant faces
of children never to be born.

I ask you to walk with me,
to watch how the trees have moved today,
their movements are divided as those of voices
and build new gardens, sweet as the limbs of children.

MORNINGS THEY COULD WALK

Mornings they could walk close to the waterfowl,
but only in the dawnlight. Her face
was that of a goddess: cold, the kind of emptiness
the heart imagines can confer grace,

but only at dawn. Tess said, "I don't know
about ghosts but . . . our souls
go outside our bodies while we are alive,"
which brought him (Angel) up short.

Herons, in the luminous mist,
were very forward, with a bold noise
as if opening doors and shutters,
entering the water,

long legs emerging from the plantation boughs,
or stood like pieces of clock-work,
turning heads and bodies on thin,
sharply bent

legs. Until the light turned her flesh
away from the godhead, the birds having fed
and the other farm hands risen from their beds.

HOW YOUR NAME WAS CARRIED

So many apples and journeys by water
that the world is the name your breath takes.
There is no sense of flesh,
nor the mind's burden of chandeliers,
diamonds, living rooms . . .
The last chair was carried through sunflowers
(the background was so dense with foliage
it seemed the one thing to get our hands on),
within the sounds of the leaves,
when the wind begins to rise
upright as the first dragon.
Water like clear bedsheets
fell down the walls from windows.
You walked clusters of bees
in the thin, bright dust. Imprint
of fronds, snowflakes, ancient weeds in amber:
more than the eye could see. The moon almost
a rose. Then the roots of the wind stiffened.
The wind separated your name more and more.

BLUE WHO

Blue mountains show us the color of space.
I watch your blue eyes look over a lake.
God, how I hate you, that's how far away you go.

Someone else has torn down the shrubs
and the trees that we knew while naked.
And, you see, the rest happens at the shoreline.

Abraham's bosom is an elevator shaft in which
you and I are leaves in the corridors of autumn.
Somehow. We do not care. About the color blue.

POEM FOR THE LAST TIME I SAW YOU

I would never have gone into that garden
without you. The spinach-green trees wedded
amongst stars in the wind. And the stars
delicate in their status as the snore
of a car on the asphalt, or the horse you'd seen
cantering in the wet meadows of a dream,
its teeth brilliant as a sunlit window,
and its lips reddened with a stream of clear spittle,
so that I said, the hell with lakes.
And longed for the curve of your neck,
as if it made sense of the garden:
its going on a paradigm for our going in.

FOLLOWING OUR LOVELIFE

When I consider love I consider your age.
Every year you have been too young or too old.
Autumn was a wash of good colors or good looks
The red leaves said: We can no longer bleed.
You are the loved one who is always deathly ill.
Your funeral leads uphill to your home.
How deep your voice has finally become.
Haunted, your arms point to alternative paths.

THE DEAD KNOCK ABOUT

The dead knock about
not only in graveyards and in beds,
shopwindows, streetlamps, photographs
serve them almost as homes.
You'll want to be their friend.

In the dark
they've gotten clumsy;
they grope and don't understand.

They've no more substance
than all the breath
your life has left.

They empty the room.
The door they open
is your own.
Without your surprise
they won't come.

ACTIVE STILL LIFE

The radiator runs our room.
We breathe what the lamp turns on.
Your shoe reports the city's street.
It's too much. So we sit and sleep.

Your eyes look back to bills and gloom.
The light turns you on to your last breath.
It's a report that your shoes walked off.
You are here as the room awakes.

WHAT IS THE FIRE?

What is on fire?
What is the fire?
Names. But they should have been stones.

We wanted the whole thing:
The hand burning as if a wintering tree,
the feet darkening with fields of weeds,
legs supporting the clouded sunburst,
arms breaking, elbows out of the fireplace.

We wanted
the whole body consumed in fire
and our hands signalling through the flame.

THE FOUR SYMBOLS AT THE FOOT OF MAP No. 28
WHICH MEAN BREAKFAST AND KEEP GOING

Once it was a crouching dog, but now it is a casket
that resembles a mask. *You are wrong. It is a cask
and it resembles a child that might become a sphinx.*

The next is a cake upon a table. *Or a straw hat over a barstool.
Or a pawn from whose nob grows the ironship Monitor.* Or a symbol.

This is a chalice that is transparent so as to disclose gold pieces.
Gold fish swim under the lid that is the pawn's head.

(We cannot agree.) This last is a cherry with hot peppers for leaves.
It is the scrotum of a god concentrated into a seed.

These are the symbols at the bottom of the map numbered 28
in the book *Gastronomical Roads of the French Provinces.*
The map shows Lourdes, Cauterets, Torbes, and to give
you an idea of the miles involved at the top left there is
a town called Belin and on the right a blue ribbon of the Garonne.
A darkness gathers. A third voice states:
You skipped the roads which bleed off the page right.
Reading downward these are: N 667, N 111, N 113, N 656, N 131,
N 654, N 130, N 124, N 643, N 21, N 632, N 129, N 117, N 618.
An arrow suggests that I "Open Here" and points left,
but I don't. The poem is all on this page.

*The poem runs off the page in two directions.
You to the left for good eats in four colors.
and I keep going to the right.*
This poem is called THE SEPARATION.
It is an egg broken that thus creates a universe.

THE OLD SITTING UP

When that door opened it slammed.
I saw that his teeth were lean,
like mirrors peeled in halves.

And the elderly sat up swiftly
from the couch, or stilled the swing
on the porch.
They reached for glasses or a glass
as if stretching themselves.
"What was that?"
And the door had slammed open.

THE SEARCH THROUGH WINTER'S GARDEN

The bird's pause in the darkened upper-
air is her exhalation.
She raises her dead child in one hand.
The unbalance of clouds is her nature.
Caught, she becomes the roots of her own tree.
We are the body of the song.
The twig prints of a crow
crossing the snow....

MIDWINTER BLOOD

These birds that we find dead in town and most often
when unexpected, as at dawn, are a form of punctuation
(if you can think of trees as fitting on the same form)
and we are led even further if their closed bodies
and the concrete steps show no blood. We have built
buildings that kill birds. They are grey mirrors
unable to example the way ice may break a tree open,
or to refer to any natural dying that might occur,
because the birds in the quiet they have come into
are grey, even where the blood also resembles dust.
This voice is grey also, without the strength to name
the grey light which fits every portion of the city.
What is lost is the punctuation. What is the name
of the bird with the streaks caused by red snow?
or by the sun, when his or her mother called?
If you were led further it would be to the wings
and to those images that fall, either angels or
the shredded pages of snow, or to the crisp curls
of leaves, hands caught in dark ice. Past the mirror
at which the bird flew and was broken is where we live
and what is needed is more and there we too are ended.

IT WAS RAINING

For Harlan

All breathing is at the border of night
and (as was your voice once) the shadows are precise,
and I wanted to hold even your hand become bone
as we did once as brothers who crossed Vernon Avenue.
Rain is how birds might share out their voice.

The radiator runs the room.
I breath what the light turns on.
My shoes record the city's streets.

You and I still hide in the hotel's corridor.

I lean on the table as if I am a mirror.
There is the thought that tomorrow
and the day that follows have passed.
Or it's a report that the shoes walked off.
I was here as the room awoke. On a net above
the bed a spider moves the way a tree limb does.
Rain fell and I thought of your ghost
as bird, as spider, and as a corridor we share.
Again, when I awoke the birds had stopped.
It rained and I recollected their scattered voice.

TOUCHING, TEARING, FALLING

By moonlight a boy tore off the *vischia*. In the bare
willow he stood on all fours curved amidst clumps
that resembled nests made by clumsy birds. When
fallen the mistletoe has the leaf of the olive
and the moon-white globe of a drained finger's tip.

To be our Christmas tree we set mistletoe
indoors in a bowl of water. When our infant son
squeezed its pale fruits they congealed on marble
like soiled drippings from a candle. And they glistened.

In Pienza the *vischia* is fixed upon walls or doors
and tied there with red ribbon. Mistletoe underlines
our need for snow, it is a message you can read
in faces and in the ground: I mean the faces
hide their joy like the earth hides the living.
At night a boy visits our willow on this business.

The white berries cannot bear an infant's touch,
which is to us so gentle, as is a snowfall indoors;
every touch is a removal and in the end harsh.
Tonight the snow falls, the willow whitens in moonlight.
I can see the boy climb out of the willow.
He does not fall, instead he shares with us the theft
that brings life, the gift that drains the living.

WE HAVE KNOWN

Tonight before the rain fell you left the porch
and the swing moves still. You were at the screen
door and the light came abrupt as the white dress
you wore by the pines. Flash of slim legs.
You left into the yellowed light of the house.

We have been a long way from town, the side doors
to homes and profiles. It has not helped to have our bodies,
except to look back on your eyes on mine and that
not even now to know, but to imply that we leave
a porch where we have known many names
as one name and forgotten the word for that.

YOU, MASKED AS THE TREE OF KNOWLEDGE

I

We have known sounds that grow.
Tonight many crickets remind us of leaves
and there is only the trunk to imagine
of that great tree.
whose voice would be swollen as the moon is,
a mouth of reflected light.

II

Let us die soon....
Indeed. It is a tree in
whose indifference we continue.

III

This becomes knowledge. Instead, I said,
"On the nakedness of their legs
roses must shudder." I meant
that I loved you finally
and wanted to call out. Night did not.
We parted. I meant your body.

IV

When the moon is tired what can we hope for.
The rest is prayer.
I must be dreaming you nightly.
The insects think so. They continue.
Let me touch you,
or let me open the window.
Stop this growth.

MOVING ALONG

From a train window hypnotized,
we observe files of wheat fields
that telegraph poles halt.

The sparrow looks up and moves off.
The sparrow flies on an old bedsheet.
This is the story of the sparrow
and of the path that is narrow.
What Hart Crane saw passing by
passes by. This is silence.

The solitary bird
pauses in our reflections.
I am talking of how to hold you
and not suffer defeat.

The image is of the newly dead.
Their arms circle our necks
and our heads. We wanted to sing
(we hurry through the turnstiles singing.)

I know the voice I wanted to use
with you, it said, "Tear
up this, its use was momentary"
(though the voice softens and states
we should reform the poem
in the folds of a bird).

HOW IT STOPPED

It might have stopped and stayed also
as a repetition of moons beneath the lindens
and the insects, whose names we do not know,
but who we think of with a grateful bending,
for they are the image of arms that move,
and it might be a country town at rest, and yet
tired children count the layers of cloud
and hold hands. Their song is close to blood.
The harvest will not occur tonight at night
and we hear songs behind the narrow street.
Somewhere there are gardens where kneeling
women speak of a man who awaits friends.
Many of them died and the fountain is quiet.
Bells, songs, a man unfolds a thin paper.
The moon draws in the ocean, flowers:
we think that it must feed on them.

We went downhill. And to celebrate our time
we learned to climb and now children hold out
their arms like the lindens' leaves in envelopes,
delicate as a string are those arms.
Broken, how the night is broken with love
and instead we are in the shadows and name them.
Now we must bring gifts, but nothing offers
itself and this way so much is owed to memory.

Nothing stops us. Fire divides us at night
and in the day we watch the sun and sleep.
Between the flames we were rested
in a cool wind calling others to join us.
We thought there was a path in darkness.
Now we laugh and there are foreign names
for imagined rocks. Give us these castles.

No questions now. After all, is there fire?
And the mix-up of ocean, Eden and youth,
cathedrals, the ubiquitous factor of youth
that states we hang on a door opening.
Hands are at ease but we need the flower
that is a drawing of a sea shore.